THE ROOTS OF INSECURITY IN HAITI

HISTORICAL CONTEXT AND INTERNATIONAL IMPLICATIONS

BEN WOOD JOHNSON, PH.D.

TESKO

TESKO PUBLISHING
www.teskopublishing.com
Middletown, Pennsylvania

TESKO PUBLISHING

TESKO PUBLISHING
(Middletown, Pennsylvania)

This book is published in French and English. The document conforms to the new spelling.

Ben Wood Johnson.

The Roots of Insecurity in Haiti: Historical Context and International Implications/by Ben Wood Johnson – first edition.

p. cm. — (Ben Wood Post)

Includes an index.

ISBN -13: 978-1-948600-46-0 (pbk.: alk. Paper)
ISBN -10: 1-948600-46-3

Format: Paperback

Also available in other formats.

1. Foreign Politics – History – United States. 2. Case studies – Caribbean and Latin America – Aims and objectives. 3. International Politics – History – Haiti. I. Johnson, Ben W. II. Title: The Roots of Insecurity in Haiti: Historical Context and International Implications.

2023

TESKO PUBLISHING, a division of My Eduka Solutions and BWEC, LLC.
If you would like to learn more about Tesko Publishing, please contact My Eduka Solutions at 330 W. Main St., Unit 214, Middletown, PA Zip 17057. Visit the website: www.teskopublishing.com.

First printed in December 2023.
Printed in the USA.

SELECTED WORKS BY BEN WOOD JOHNSON

DEDICATION

In memory of my good friend,
Germain "Ti Fleur" Saint Fleur.
Your life ended too soon my
brother (RIP).

CONTENTS

PREFACE

Let me begin this book by echoing what most sound-minded observers might consider a thought-provoking statement. That is, Haiti is not a failed state. But what argument could convincingly support that assertion? There is a simple and clear explanation for this claim. That is, Haiti is not a state; at least it no longer enjoys such a status.

Haiti is [effectively] an occupied land with a semblance of governance and authority. In reality, the place is completely controlled by foreign entities, specifically the United States. For these reasons, calling Haiti a failed state embodies one's intransigence or one's ignorance about the territory once known as the Republic of Haiti.

Let me echo that the previous avowal was not designed to signify a surrender of Haiti. The fight to save Haiti has just begun. It will not end until the land, which Haitians have earned from sweat and blood, has been restored to their rightful owners: Haitians themselves. Granted, it is going to be an arduous struggle. But Haiti's intricate history is interlaced with narratives of resilience, struggles, and a continuous quest for nationhood.

Each facet of the country's reality is characterized by the socio-political dynamics that have shaped its present state. This is to say that all is not lost for Haiti. The mere fact that you are reading this book epitomizes that reality in its most tangible sense. Haiti will never die.

Before we go further in this narrative, let me thank you for picking up this tome. This work, brief though it is, was concocted hoping to refute existing worldviews about Haiti. The common inclination is to refer to Haiti as a "Failed State." But no one has ever said, at least not out loud, who deserves the blame for Haiti's distress, namely its perceived bad luck or even the country's actual misfortunes on the world stage. They say that Haiti is a failed experiment. Is that truly the case? Here is the truth.

Since its creation, the country has been plagued by turmoil and political disarray. One could also make the argument that this reality has been a strategy concocted to keep both Haiti and Haitians distracted from their true purpose in the Western Hemisphere. Haiti was never designed to be the renegade of the American continent. It was quite the opposite. That is why, to this day, no other nations in the region have accomplished Haiti's feat. They simply do not have the wit to be like Haiti.

Haitians are the leaders of the world. We embody perfection and valor. We are the most vivid examples of the human spirit. Yet, we are vilified as if we were worthless pieces of human wastes. In fact, we have been referred to as such.[1]

In the academic realm, Haitian affairs have been relegated to a trivial prospect. Haitian politics has no empirical merit. In certain circles, Haitian intellect has no value beyond that attached to it by perverted liberal minds or pseudo-thinkers who have convinced themselves that they are not only smarter than the average Haitian, but it is also their sacred mission to save Haitians from themselves or to save Haiti from Haitians. Nonetheless, this is far from the truth, as these people are self-anointed and drowning in their hubris while being entrenched in self-pity and a senseless depravity. Haitians are much worthier than they are.

Here is another depressing reality; Haitians are labeled a certain way, which seldom does justice to their true nature. For instance, the term "poverty" is often equated to being Haitian. Other demeaning terms include "Boat people," "immigrants," "violent," "gang," "cannibals," and "corrupt," among other derogatory appellations or disparaging epithets. Hence, the distinction between the

[1] In 2018, President Donald J. Trump, they say, referred to Haiti as a shi*hole country. Whether these words were actually uttered by Mr. Trump himself has never been proven beyond a reasonable doubt. Still, the popular presumption is that Haiti is worthless; Haitians are worthless. Read more here:
https://www.pbs.org/newshour/politics/trump-denies-he-used-profane-language-to-describe-african-countries;
https://www.cnn.com/2018/01/11/politics/immigrants-shithole-countries-trump/index.html

land and its people is often too blurred to even account for in the conversation. From most people's vantage point, Haitians have no humanity; they have no intrinsic human valor worthy of recognition.

What used to be echoed and even whispered about Haiti and Haitians in dark alleys and narrow corridors are being proclaimed out in the open. The internet is littered with anti-Haitian sentiments. It is always fascinating to read online comments from individuals who have no sense of history. Yet, they feel entitled to teach Haitians how to conduct themselves in the world. Many of these misguided souls cannot comprehend that Haitians are in the struggle of their existence. The mere fact that Haiti is still standing is evidence of the Haitian people's valiant determination not to surrender their land to the neocolonialists of our time.

To say it again, Haiti will never die. So long as there is at least one Haitian alive, so will Haiti, so will the land, and so will its history. Sadly, it is not always possible to defend Haiti, specifically in the intellectual realm, given that the country has many flaws, some of which are often used as evidence of its inherent decadence or shortcoming as a state or as a nation. Here, nonetheless, the aim is to rebut erroneous arguments against Haiti by assessing the roots of insecurity in that part of the world.

The term "Failed State," at least within the context of international parlance, denotes a political entity, which is characterized by a central government so feeble or ineffective that it has little practical control over much of its territory; it cannot provide public services, which makes that state illegitimate. Therefore, the state or the country itself is not recognized as an authentic entity by the international community. Granted, this is Haiti's status, albeit not overtly, within the international system.

The present edition offers a holistic exploration of Haiti's reality, be it political, societal, or economic. It lingers on ideas echoed in the literature linking Haiti (the country) and Haiti (its people) as a failed enterprise. This dialogue is based on the erroneous application of the concept known as "Failed State" to Haiti's current status within the international political spectrum. Haiti's situation, I will argue here, is much direr than being equated as a failed state. Haiti's conditions, I will further denote, are much more subjugated than anyone could imagine. In fact, Haiti is currently in a foreign occupation. I will use recent events in Haiti's political history to support my arguments.

Despite the broad nature of the contentions echoed in this compilation, the focus is on the cause of the chaos that has become a part of Haitian DNA over the last few years, if not the last three decades. While many texts have delved into the topic, this book seeks to offer a unique perspective in the debate, given that it is the intellectual brainchild of a son of Haiti. The book, in all its simplicity, examines Haiti's historical context from the prism of someone who has lived part of that history. In doing so, the text relates the international implications of the country's current state of disarray.

Haiti's history is a captivating study. It encompasses the daring defiance of a slave revolt against their colonial masters. The birth of the Haitian nation was a defiance to existing norms. Since that major accomplishment, Haiti has found itself in a continuous struggle to retain its fundamental rights to exist around neighbors that seem determined to deny the country its inalienable right to exist on its own and for its own. Hence, Haiti is repeatedly denied the right to self-determination. The Haitian people, amid this tragedy, are against the oppressive forces both within and outside their borders.

Haiti's history is also marred by instances of foreign intrusions. External socio-economic and political forces have shaped the country's destiny. The aftermath of Haiti's independence in 1804 and the assassination of the country's first head of state, Jean-Jacques Dessalines, led to international isolation, which also led to a series of political turmoil. Over the years, that reality has beleaguered the nation.

The influence of international politics is a fundamental aspect of the Haitian narrative. It is important to examine the influence of the Monroe Doctrine, which asserted the United States' hegemony in the Western Hemisphere. It is also pertinent to review the noted doctrine's impact on Haiti's political and economic realities, including the country's international isolation, the crippling economic sanctions, and the continual interference of foreign powers. These realities have played a significant role in shaping Haiti's present state, which many consider a complete failure by any measures, though this is not Haiti's fault.

The book explores the reality of human security in Haiti, an understanding that encompasses the various aspects of security, which are necessary for individuals and communities to live in freedom, peace, and safety. Haiti's history is marked by persistent insecurity, with its citizens continually grappling with political instability, economic hardship, and social inequality. These issues necessitate a thorough examination of the domestic and international policies, which have contributed to Haiti's current state of recurrent insecurity.

As you navigate the next few pages, bear in mind that the aim of this book is not to pathologize Haiti. However, it is essential to provide a nuanced understanding of the factors that have led to the country's continual status within the international community. The hope is to stimulate a discourse, which moves beyond the simplistic narrative of Haiti as a "failed state." The book was conceived with the sole design of helping readers embrace the complexity of Haiti's history, which is characterized by the resilience of its people and the potential for its future.

Considering the empirical nature of this book, it is intended for scholars, students, and anyone interested in Caribbean politics, policing, international security, and development studies. It is an invitation to journey through the pages of Haiti's history. The book is also a call to engage in critical dialogue about the international implications of Haiti's current state.

As you embark on this literary escapade, the hope is that the arguments and the insights echoed here will help illuminate the intricacies of Haiti's past, present, and future. Another hope is that the book will incite a deeper understanding of the myriad factors, which have shaped and, some might say, have continued to influence Haiti, a country that some observers might label fascinating, yet a misunderstood nation. Join me in this promenade through the halls of Haiti's political history.

Ben Wood Johnson, Ph.D.

Pennsylvania, USA
December 2023

Minimal update (March 2024)

INTRODUCTION

Haiti is constantly meandering between a state of complete social chaos and political anarchy. Skirmishes among competing political factions have rendered the Haitian state moribund and nearly inexistent. This reality has perpetuated a climate of violence, which is characterized by organized criminality, gang proliferation, and the lack of law and order. This state of fact has placed Haiti among the failed states in the world.

Plague by its stoic history, international interventions, political instability, criminality, and socio-economic factors, Haiti has never been able to transcend from the first black republic in the World to an un-encroached and independent society. By relying on a qualitative method known as process tracing, this work explores the underlying causes and implications of insecurity in Haiti. However, the focus is on the nation's relationship with the international community.

By examining key events, such as the assassination of President Jovenel Moïse, the book sheds light on Haiti's vulnerability and the convoluted nature of its global ties. The book also delves into the influence of the Monroe Doctrine on Haiti's political landscape, highlighting the struggle for sovereignty amidst foreign interventions. The role of media in exacerbating Haiti's insecurity is investigated, specifically through the case of the kidnapped American missionaries and its worldwide consequences.

The analysis featured here exposes the unsettling reality of these abductions and their profound impact on Haiti's social fabric. Haiti's current state of fear and the widespread of criminality are a direct outcome of historical and systemic factors, which are aggravated by the international community's actions and inactions. While emphasizing the need for a thorough understanding of Haiti's historical context, the book calls for a coordinated, but also a well-informed international approach, to addressing the complex challenges faced by this bourgeoning nation.

CHAPTER 1

PRESUMPTION: HAITI IS A FAILED STATE

The present security crisis in Haiti has historical implications. There is no doubt that the country is in a deepening state of emergency. Haitians are experiencing a crisis the like of which the country has never seen before. Seemingly, that state of affairs is by design.

At the moment, Haiti is without a president, which is, by tradition, the trademark of the Haitian state itself. But all indications suggest that the country's current situation results from a global project, as various countries within the international community have seemingly made it so that Haiti remains subservient to their political emprises. Thus, the country is neither governed nor administered.

The presumption is that Haiti is a "failed state." Does that mean that Haiti is indeed a failure of a state, and deservingly so, some might add? I would say not at all. In fact, Haiti is a state that they have failed and for panoply of reasons. We could debate the nature of who is "They" in the present context. But if you were to pose this question to Haitians, most people in that part of the world would reply with an utmost certainty: Se blan ki kraze Ayiti. Translation: "The white men have broken Haiti." Sadly, there is ample evidence in the halls of the country's history to support that apprehension. But before we delve in the crux of the debate, it is important to revisit the underpinnings of the concept understood as state failure.

Let me restate the previous question: is Haiti truly a failed state? Well, some pundits seem convinced that the answer is irrefutably in the affirmative, particularly given recent events, which saw the country's prime minister, Mr. Ariel Henry, grounded in Puerto Rico, unable to return home due to gang violence (John et al., 2024; E. Sanon et al., 2024). Let me also say that it is intellectually captivating to hear or to watch so-called experts talking about Haiti as if they know what is truly going on there. Let me be a little bit pompous: these people, for the most part, have no clue as to the roots of the real situation in Haiti. As well, those who do know a little bit about what is happening in Haiti are likely to omit the truth to further a particular narrative expressly or else because of their false sense of virtue about their role in Haitian affairs.

Without giving away the juicy titbits about the arguments, which you will soon uncover as you thumb through the next few chapters, Haiti is the victim of a vast conspiracy designed to keep it in a stagnant state of continuous fiasco, which, evidently, also gives rise to a perpetual need for foreign interventions. In essence, Haiti has lost its rights to self-determination. Haitians are at the mercy of powerful forces, many of whom have an important stake in the administrative paucity of the land. Then again, is Haiti a failed state? Is it a failing state? Or is it a state being failed on purpose? Of course, the implications of each question could leave you bewildered.

Presently, Haiti is ruled by pockets of gangsters, many of whom threaten civil war (Buschschlüter, 2024). There is no effective government in the country; observers are wondering "how it got so bad" (Ioanes, 2024). Is that proof enough that the Haiti is indeed a failed state? I will return to this question and others like it, which had been posed earlier in this section later in the text. For now, let me say that the term "failed state" generally refers to a nation-state that is embarrassingly unable to sustain itself as a member of the international community (Gould, 2014). This definition emphasizes the failure of the state to function effectively within the global community. However, it is also relevant to note that the label "failed state," in and of itself, is contentious and problematic, considering that it has the potential to stifle efforts to understand the complex social phenomena that contribute to state failure (Hameiri, 2007). The complexities of state failure can be rooted in global or regional processes. This is not merely a problem of the state itself.

The issue of state failure is often understood based on a nation's inability to develop. Thus, the term is closely linked to development, particularly in terms of political and socio-economic realities. Under such an unblemished prism, development is seen as a crucial means of resolving the challenges associated with failed states (Tantua & Isukul, 2022). When a state is unable to develop, it exhibits signs of social and/or political stagnation, which are characterized by failed social institutions and other apparatus. However, the internal constraints within failing states can impede reform efforts, making it difficult to address the underlying issues contributing to state failure (Chauvet & Collier, 2008).

The concept of state failure has also been associated with the idea of sovereignty and the capacity of the state to engage in collaboration. Observers use the term "shadow of hierarchy" to refer to the state's capacity for collaboration, which is relevant for understanding weak or failed states (Jessop, 2015). But the discourse on failed states has highlighted the challenges of state restructuring and the future of the state as a fundamental institution (Eriksen, 2011). The conversation on failed states has often raised questions about the sustainability and future of unrecognized quasi-states, which have also emphasized the complexities of statehood and recognition in the international system (Kolstø, 2006).

The idea of state failure is deeply intertwined with the broader discussions on sovereignty, institutions, and the contradictions of state formation (Sørensen, 1999). Do these realities apply to Haiti? The answer may be mitigated, given the historical woes of the Haitian state and the lack of agency of Haitian leaders in Haitian affairs.

CHAPTER 2

UNDERSTANDING THE HISTORICAL CONTEXT

Since the tragic death of Jovenel Moïse in 2021, the country's duly elected head of state, Haiti has found itself in a state of a sociopolitical freefall. The deepening state of emergency, which has become the identity of the Haitian state, is demoralizing. Sadly, the Haitian people are paying the price. The country is grappling with a critical state of emergency in terms of security.

In 2022, the United Nations Office for the Coordination of Humanitarian Affairs highlights a troubling increase in gang violence in Haiti, targeting civilians since 2021, with violent confrontations between rival gangs escalating at an alarming rate. The summer of 2021 marked a turning point, as the socioeconomic landscape in Port-au-Prince became increasingly dominated by these violent clashes (UN Office for the Coordination of Humanitarian Affairs, 2022). To better grasp the root causes of this security crisis in Haiti, it is essential to recognize that the pervasive insecurity, which has become the trademark of this struggling Caribbean nation, is not a recent development but rather a long-standing issue.

To reiterate a pervious assertion, Haiti has long been plagued by popular uprisings, violence, and political instability. The international community, particularly the United Nations, has been actively involved in the country since 1994. However, their role in Haitian affairs increased in 2004, after the international community, notably the US, France, and Canada, overthrew Jean-Bertrand Aristide, Haiti duly elected president. This abrupt political development led many in Haiti to fight against the foreign occupation, which the UN spearheaded unrepentantly, despite the evidence to suggest this misguided endeavor had been a complete failure.

In 2006, open conflict erupted between UN forces and armed militias in Port-au-Prince (Ponsar et al., 2009). By 2014, the United Nations Stabilization Mission in Haiti (MINUSTAH) had targeted local gangs (Cockayne, 2014). However, their efforts were unsuccessful. While peacekeeping operations in Haiti have had an impact on humanitarian initiatives, they have not produced the desired outcomes in terms of security (Sauter, 2022). For many Haitians, the MINUSTAH represented an unwelcome foreign presence with questionable legitimacy (Ciorciari, 2022), which they vowed to fight against by any means necessary and at any costs.

Over time, Haitian gangs have evolved and strengthened, becoming increasingly formidable in their criminal endeavors. They have become more powerful strategic local actors and are beginning to expand their activities across the country (Cockayne, 2014; Olivier, 2021). Haitian gang members are criminals who, over the years, mutated from political armed groups to criminals who perpetrated incommensurable violence in the country (Schuberth, 2015). They now possess more sophisticated weaponry. They exhibit a heightened determination to cause harm to Haitian society. Their levels of violence have reached unprecedented heights. Granted, the issue of gang-related insecurity has been brewing in Haiti for years, with its roots extending deep into the country's complex history.

To address the current state of emergency in Haiti, it is crucial to examine the broader historical and socio-political context, which has given rise to the current security crisis in the country. This includes understanding the role of the international community, the efficacy of past interventions, and the factors that have contributed to the growing power and violence of Haitian gangs. It is vital to comprehend the complexities of the situation in Haiti. It is important to work towards finding viable solutions to mitigate the ongoing security crisis in the country.

CHAPTER 3

ASSESSING THE NGO FACTOR

In general, NGOs, or non-governmental organizations, have been a subject of debate regarding their impact on poverty in developing countries. Proponents argue that NGOs play a crucial role in poverty alleviation by providing aid, implementing innovative models, and addressing critical issues such as healthcare, education, and economic empowerment (Ferdous, 2014; Sillah & Adesopo, 2022; Vinaygathasan & Pallegedara, 2014). They are seen as essential actors in delivering aid programs for poverty alleviation and are often perceived as more trustworthy than recipient governments in terms of fund utilization, particularly in countries with corruption problems and poor governance systems (Chu & Luke, 2022; Saeng Outhay, 2015). Similarly, NGOs are credited with reaching the poorest of the poor and successfully reducing poverty in some developing countries (Sillah & Adesopo, 2022; Vinaygathasan & Pallegedara, 2014).

However, the debate is raging as to the real impact of NGOs on poor or developing countries.

Critics argue that the effectiveness of NGOs in poverty reduction is often contested. As a result, their relationships in developing countries are often characterized by competition rather than cooperation (Gugerty, 2008). There are concerns that donor funding to NGOs in developing countries may be creating a new elite within civil society, which is more aligned with the interests of foreign donors than with the local population (Bano, 2008). But other claims against NGOs denote that poverty reduction has slowed or even reversed in various nations, despite the continued efforts of NGOs and others to address poverty (Chu & Luke, 2021). This somber panoramic view of NGOs is not different from the reality on the ground in Haiti.

The consensus is that NGOs have not been good for Haiti's long-term progress. Put differently, the presence of foreign entities in Haiti does not bode well for the country. The international community has a complex relationship with Haiti. For years, Haiti has experienced an influx of foreign activities, primarily driven by Non-Governmental Organizations (NGOs).

While these organizations have played a crucial role in humanitarian aid (Ryfman, 2007), they have also left a lasting, negative impact on the country, such as the spread of cholera (Hendel et al., 2022). Largely dependent on aid because of limited domestic production, Haiti has become increasingly reliant on foreign entities for survival

(Ceccorulli & Coticchia, 2016). The presence of these organizations has also led to unintended consequences, including a surge in criminality.

Over the course of its history, the international community has affected Haiti negatively (Farmer et al., 2005). With the role that NGOs play in Haiti, the line between invasion or infusion is blurry (Schuller, 2007). The influx of foreign nationals into Haiti has opened the door for a variety of illicit activities, such as human trafficking, drug trafficking, and other vices.

NGOs are not good for Haiti (Bebbington et al., 2007). They have either replaced state institutions or have fragilized existing ones (Zanotti, 2010), which consequence is to undermine a state's governance capacity (Schuller, 2009). As a result, Haitian criminals have become more sophisticated, in part because of their connections with foreign entities that supply them with advanced weaponry and expertise to wreak havoc in Haitian society.

NGOs have had a mixed impact on both Haiti and its people, contributing to the emergence of new economic actors and changes in the Haitian diet (Van Engeland, 2016). Hindered by a lack of coordination, their efforts have often fallen short in providing effective humanitarian aid (Anders, 2013). But it would be unfair to blame foreign entities solely for the country's criminal woes.

Haiti's long history of insecurity has various roots, with some observers attributing this reality to foreign interventions, such as the US occupation of the country in

1915. Others argue that the instability stems from the nation's ongoing political volatility, resulting from Haitians' inability to unite and to adopt policies that serve the best interests of the country. Critics have contended that the pervasive insecurity that seems entrenched within Haitian society is ontological in nature (James, 2003).

Regardless of the perceived root cause of Haiti's insecurity, the consequences of the phenomenon are undeniably detrimental to both the country and its people. It is essential to consider the complex interplay among foreign entities, NGOs, and domestic factors to better understand and address the ongoing security crisis in Haiti. There is a need to develop a more comprehensive understanding of the situation in Haiti. It is important to explore potential solutions that consider the roles of various stakeholders, both foreign and domestic.

CHAPTER 4

THE GLOBAL IMPACT OF HAITI'S INSECURITY

The persistent state of insecurity that plagues Haiti is not novel. This reality has frequently led to foreign military interventions, which have proved detrimental to both the Haitian state and its people (James, 2009). It is central to consider the broader implications of Haiti's insecurity, as the issue extends beyond the country's borders. It has the potential to become a regional, if not global, security threat to nations across the Americas. Addressing this problem head-on is imperative.

Despite its challenges, Haiti remains an independent state. Its people deserve the same rights and dignity as any other nation. The Haitian state has inalienable rights, including the right to exist, the right to self-determination, and the right to engage in trade and diplomacy with other countries. Regardless of its economic standing or regional influence, Haiti is a legitimate entity; it holds the power and authority to interact with various states worldwide.

Unquestionably, extensive lawlessness plagues the Haitian state. The country has been grappling with general gang violence, which has been exacerbated by a multitude of factors, including, but not limited to civil and political unrest, natural disasters, coups, political leader assassinations, gang/organized crime, uprisings, and rapid political turnovers (Vahedi et al., 2021). The lack of security and protection in internally displaced persons camps, combined with inadequate living conditions and a lack of police patrols, has elevated exposure to violence, particularly gender-based violence, and has created precarious living situations for internally displaced persons in Haiti (Logie et al., 2017).

Punitive attitudes toward crime in Haiti, as well as in other Caribbean countries, may result from mass media's disproportionate focus on violent crime, which can exacerbate public fear and panic (Limoncelli et al., 2020). The situation in Haiti has led to significant risks of violence against women, as documented by several international organizations following the 2010 earthquake (Killion et al., 2018). But the impact of economic sanctions on health and health systems in low-income and middle-income countries, including Haiti, has led to coping strategies, such as changes in dietary habits, urban-to-rural migration, and disruption of family formation (Pintor et al., 2023). The necessity of international cooperation has sparked debates on issues of integration and solidarity with the people of Haiti, particularly in the context of agricultural development against hunger and poverty (Exime et al., 2021).

The security situation in Haiti has also drawn comparisons with other contexts. For instance, a point of strife is centered on the challenges United Nations peacekeeping operations faced, where the termination of operations in Haiti has been highlighted because of ongoing pressure from significant financial donors to cut expenditures in current operations, especially in areas suffering severe political and security issues (Nordin et al., 2022). Another example is a comparison between Gambia and Haiti, which reveals differences in both situations, shedding light on the complexities of state sovereignty and foreign intervention (Beatrice, 2019).

There is no debate about this reality; Haiti is under the influence of individuals with criminal tendencies, some of whom, many are convinced, are state officials. This situation has resulted in continuous violations of the law, which have far-reaching implications, potentially impacting both regional and international partners negatively. Hence, the growing threat of Haitian criminal elements could not be understated. Its international impact can be undeniable.

Haiti's criminal elements are becoming increasingly urbanized and dangerous. Their actions often transcend mere political statements. These individuals pose a significant risk to global peace and international security, particularly when considering US homeland security concerns.

The ongoing insecurity in Haiti has forced many families to leave their homes. At the same time, others are driven away by poverty, food insecurity, and economic difficulties. The 2021 earthquake and the country's volatile political climate have led many Haitians to seek a better life elsewhere, as evidenced by the situation at the Mexican/US border in 2021 (Diaz-Bonilla, 2022, p. 10). Considering these multiple misfortunes, there is a pressing need for further actions, which the author characterized as "the need for a strong response now" to address the situation in Haiti (Diaz-Bonilla, 2022, p. 20).

The security implications of Haiti's rampant criminality could have far-reaching and complex regional consequences. Neighboring countries such as the Dominican Republic, Jamaica, Puerto Rico, and the Bahamas are particularly vulnerable to the negative effects of Haitian gang activities. The international community must recognize the strengthening of Haitian criminal elements. It must acknowledge the rise of insecurity in Haiti as a serious matter that extends beyond the country's borders.

Addressing the insecurity issue within the Haitian State is vital. However, the security problem in Haiti is a complex and multifaceted challenge; it encompasses various aspects, such as public health, political stability, and social cohesion.

The country has faced significant public health challenges, including the outbreak of cholera, which prompted the implementation of mass oral cholera vaccination programs (Deen et al., 2016). The state's fragility has been a barrier to achieving lasting changes in economic, political, and social conditions, which are essential for addressing security concerns (Feldmann et al., 2011). As articulated earlier, the historical context of racialized violence, such as the 1937 massacre of people of Haitian origin in the Dominican Republic, has contributed to the complex security landscape in the region (Howard, 2007).

In the aftermath of the 2010 earthquake, Haiti's security and development have been intertwined, with the country being a focal point for humanitarian aid and peacekeeping efforts, an aid. Ironically, Raoul Peck, the famous Haitian-born filmmaker, classified the international aid to Haiti during the post-earthquake era as "Fatal Assistance," (Dargis, 2014; Peck, 2013), considering the unintended effects of the international support to Haiti.[2] The interconnectedness of security and development is clear in the challenges faced by the Haitian

---

[2] Raoul Peck is a famous Haitian-born filmmaker. He explored the effects of the assistance the international community provided to Haiti in the aftermath of the 2010 earthquake. See these links to learn more:
https://www.nytimes.com/2014/02/28/movies/fatal-assistance-about-relief-efforts-in-haiti.html;
https://www.imdb.com/title/tt2373878/

State, as stability operations have been necessary alongside conventional skills (Black, 2013). But the country's vulnerability to natural disasters, such as hurricanes and earthquakes, has further compounded its security challenges, which has also increased the need for a comprehensive approach to resilience-building and disaster preparedness (Bazin & Saintis, 2021).

The transnational ties maintained by Haitian immigrants have also played a role in addressing health issues, as they have used connections with their home country to buy medical supplies and support for their communities in the U.S. (M.-A. Sanon et al., 2014). This reality highlights the interconnectedness of security issues between Haiti and its diaspora communities, emphasizing the need for a transnational approach to security and well-being. The crisis in Haiti's security calls for a multidimensional approach, a method that combines traditional and innovative security measures (Rodrigues, 2015). The intertwining of security and justice development programming has been a crucial aspect of addressing the security challenges in fragile situations, including Haiti (van Veen, 2016). The country's recognition of education as a crucial part of sustainable development and resilience-building also underscores the multifaceted nature of addressing security concerns (Bazin & Saintis, 2021).

It is important to rethink the realities on the ground in Haiti. However, doing so requires a comprehensive approach, which considers the interests of not only the

Haitian people but also other nations in the Western Hemisphere. Concerted efforts from all parties are central to mitigating the threat posed by Haiti's growing criminal elements. Therefore, Haiti's security problems could not be solved in a vacuum. It is important to enhance the security of the entire region.

To address the security crisis in Haiti effectively, it is essential to understand the complex interplay among local, regional, and international factors. This includes examining the roles and the responsibilities of the Haitian state, its people, and foreign entities in contributing to the current state of insecurity in that part of the world. To develop a comprehensive assessment of the situation in Haiti, it is vital to explore potential solutions that consider the interests of various stakeholders at multiple levels. Only through a holistic approach can we hope to make lasting progress in addressing Haiti's security challenges and their broader ramifications.

Here is the depressing truth; it does not seem like there is a sense of urgency to address Haiti's security woes. The logical question is: who then benefits from Haiti's current state of disarray? The answer might surprise you, as Haitians have no stake in the insecurity that plagues their nation and stifles the country's development. Another logical question is why has the international community allowed the situation to get so bad in Haiti? Well, the answer might seem conspiratorial. Perhaps the next few chapters might help shed some light on these questions.

CHAPTER 5

THE DEATH OF A SITTING PRESIDENT

Over the last few years or so, Haiti has garnered significant media attention. Through various media outlets, the country has captivated audiences both nationally and internationally. The primary catalyst for this increased coverage in Haitian affairs in the Western media was the daring assassination of President Jovenel Moïse, which occurred on July 7, 2021.

The known details of the murder show that a group consisting primarily of foreign assailants infiltrated the president's private residence, located on the outskirts of the capital, during the night. They killed President Moïse and wounded his wife, Martine Moïse (Porter et al., 2021). According to high-ranking Haitian officials, including then-Police Chief Leon Charles, many of the individuals involved in the attack were "mercenaries" and "assassins"

(Fils-Aime & Charles, 2021), some of whom were reportedly hired from Colombia. However, that is not all.

Other investigations have revealed potential connections to the US, as many of the assailants (or those affiliated with them) had ties to the country. The security company responsible for hiring the individuals involved in the assassination is based in Florida. It is registered to operate in the US.

The American government's response to the Haitian president assassination's aftermath has raised suspicions. Various observers were convinced that the president's demise was effectively a soft coup, which had been spearheaded by both internal and external forces to depose President Moïse, considering the events that unfolded soon after the assassination. For instance, there has not been a genuine attempt to uncover the truth vis-à-vis what led to President's Moïse's death. Plus, the Haitian justice system is in disarray.

Currently, no reform is on the way to address the failings of the Haitian justice system, which raises more concerns about a possible conspiracy to gaslight what really took place at the president's home the night of his assassination. This plausibility, though not unfounded, has led some observers to believe that there may be a cover-up attempting to conceal the involvement of American officials in the killing of the Haitian president. But this likelihood is despicable.

The foreign media interests in Haitian affairs and, at the same time, the apparent lack of enthusiasm to ask questions about what truly transpired at the presidential compound has given traction to the presumption that American officials, at the highest level of the American government, may have played a role in the president's demise. In the same way, the likely involvement of foreign entities in the assassination of President Jovenel Moïse has not been challenged. The political reality on the ground in Haiti also supports such a suspicion, considering that Haitians are unable to choose their leader, which reinforced the belief that a coup occurred in Haiti the day that Jovenel Moïse was declared dead. Since then, Haiti has been placed on a political diet, which only serves the international community, namely the United States. It goes without saying that American officials have single-handedly benefited from President Moïse's death, a reality that supports the notion of a soft coup d'état in Haiti.

As the investigation into the death of the president continues and new information comes to light, it is important to examine the roles and responsibilities of various stakeholders at local, regional, and international levels critically. A comprehensive understanding of the situation in Haiti is necessary. A thorough assessment of the involvement of external actors is congruently crucial to ensure transparency, accountability, and justice for the Haitian people.

While there are suspicions concerning the role that the US might have played in the President's assassination, a move by American officials has raised further questions about the situation in Haiti. Ariel Henry, a person suspected of being involved in President Moïse's killing, was chosen by American government officials to succeed him. The common understanding is that Henry was involved in the assassination's planning or else he has a close link with the person believed to be the mastermind of the president's killing (Abi-Habib & Kurmanaev, 2021; Gallón et al., 2022). The decision to place Henry at the helm of Haiti's political pinnacle, especially as prime minister, is deemed illegal under the Haitian constitution. Yet, despite Henry's lack of legitimacy and popularity, he remains America's strong man in Haiti.

Notwithstanding claims to the contrary, American officials have not shown a genuine interest in uncovering the truth behind President Moïse's murder. Their apparent hypocrisy has not gone unnoticed by the Haitian people and other observers. Considering that the US Ambassador Michele Sison, who presented her credentials to President Moïse in 2018 (U. S. Mission Haiti, 2018), lived close to the crime scene, it seems unlikely that the American government was not aware of the events that occurred in Haiti. In what various observers consider an attempt to control the narrative surrounding the assassination, American officials have taken several people under investigation by the Haitian police into their custody under the guise of pursuing justice.

Despite significant media revelations by outlets such as CNN and the New York Times about the potential role Ariel Henry may have played in the assassination, the American government has remained silent on the matter.

Perhaps, as intended, this silence has reinforced Mr. Henry's power and authority in the impoverished Caribbean nation. Under Henry's rule, Haiti has become dominated by pockets of gangsters, which various observers believe to be under the control of Prime Minister Henry himself and his foreign supporters, including the Americans.

The potential complicity of American officials in President Moïse's untimely death seems increasingly plausible. This reality has cast a shadow of doubt over international efforts to help the country recuperate from its ongoing crises and political turmoil, including the rise in criminality, gang violence, kidnapping, and other societal issues. The US handling of the situation in Haiti has led some critics to raise questions about the roles and responsibilities of international actors in the climate of insecurity that dominate the Haitian society.

CHAPTER 6

HAITI AND THE MONROE DOCTRINE

The US has long exerted considerable influence in the Caribbean, often treating the region as its own backyard. The Haitian revolution redefined the "master-slave" relations within the bowels of the French empire (Ghachem, 2012), which ushered in a movement of denial of revolutionary antislavery, which also became the centerpiece of a range of hegemonic thought (Fischer, 2004; Lewis, 2004). But the Haitian revolution provoked distinct reactions both in the old and the new world order, while reverberating in other parts of the Caribbean, notably in Cuba (Geggus & Fiering, 2009; Rebok, 2009).

The Monroe Doctrine became the articulation of US goals and purposes in the Western Hemisphere (Gilderhus, 2006). Other than financial and economic fallouts, countries that fell under the realm of similar policies have seen their political autonomy utterly weakened (Pillet, 1914). Invoking the Monroe Doctrine, American officials have consistently displayed their intent to control the political affairs of every country in the region, with the ultimate aim of preserving their national security interests.

Historical events, such as the Cuban Missile Crisis in October 1962, serve as prime examples of America's determination to maintain a stronghold in the Caribbean. It would be naïve to assume that the US does not exercise considerable control over various actions, omissions, or incidents taking place in the Americas, including in Caribbean states like Haiti. Historically, the Monroe Doctrine has been used as a guide for US involvement in Latin America and the Caribbean (Dent, 1999). It has also influenced Haiti's foreign policy (Dent, 1999).

Given the circumstances surrounding President Jovenel Moïse's assassination and the fact that the conspiracy is believed to have originated on US soil, three plausible scenarios merit consideration. The first possibility is that the US National Security Agency (NSA) severely failed in its intelligence capabilities by not uncovering the plot to assassinate a foreign (friendly) head of state on US soil. Under this assumption, President Moïse's assassination would be viewed as a random act that Haitian security forces, regional security entities, and the US intelligence community could neither predict nor prevent. However, this option seems unlikely.

The second possibility suggests that American officials were aware of the plot to kill the Haitian president but chose to ignore it, as doing so aligned with their foreign policy objectives in Haiti. While this scenario may be more plausible, it remains somewhat unrealistic, as American officials would likely anticipate the diplomatic repercussions that they might face and the need to provide explanations for their actions. Therefore, this scenario may not fully capture the true nature of events leading up to President Moïse's assassination.

The third scenario considers the possibility that President Moïse's assassination was premeditated and driven by his geopolitical choices. This setup considers Moïse's recent trip to Turkey and potential partnerships with Russia to develop Haiti in various sectors, such as energy and infrastructure. Under this assumption, the assassination could result from a calculated move to punish Moïse for his expected geopolitical alliances, which may have threatened US interests in the region.

The intricate web of US influence in Haiti raises critical questions about the country's role in the region and its potential involvement in shaping the political landscape of Caribbean nations, including Haiti. As we evaluate the different scenarios that may have contributed to President Moïse's assassination, it is essential to recognize the broader implications of US power and control in the Caribbean. The US role in Haitian politics can be irrefutable.

An additional, but not entirely implausible, scenario suggests that the plot to assassinate President Moïse was an integral part of the US agenda for Haiti from the beginning. Unfortunately, President Moïse may not have been politically astute enough to recognize this possibility. It is conceivable that he lacked the guidance of knowledgeable political advisors or foreign policy experts who could have expected such an outcome, particularly given the US's apparent support for Moïse despite his dictatorial tendencies and the Haitian people's rejection of his politics. It is worth noting that Moïse's political approach was influenced in part by foreign actors, including shortsighted individuals from the American State Department and the United Nations. Undoubtedly, each of these potential scenarios is deeply unsettling.

The circumstances of President Moïse's death are disheartening. It appears increasingly improbable that the truth behind his assassination will ever be revealed. The Haitian people may never learn who was responsible for their president's death. If this uncertainty is not indicative of US involvement in Moïse's killing, it is difficult to imagine what else could be, as Haiti has long been under US tutelage.

With the Haitian justice system in disarray, the Haitian national police are effectively beholden to the whims of the US ambassador in Haiti. Those in power in Haiti may be complicit in the ongoing turmoil that plagues the nation. Given the US's extensive influence in Haiti, it is difficult for American officials to deny their responsibility for the persistent instability that has characterized the country for over three decades. As we continue to explore the potential role of the US in shaping Haiti's political landscape and the assassination of President Moïse, it is essential to consider the broader implications of American influence in the Caribbean region and its possible ramifications for nations like Haiti.

CHAPTER 7

THE UNEXPLAINED VULNERABILITY OF A PRESIDENT

The shocking assassination of Jovenel Moïse caught many observers off guard, as it was a brazen attack on a sitting president. This event should have been a cause for alarm for regional heads of state. However, Luis Abinader, the president of the Dominican Republic, which shares a border with Haiti, seemed largely unperturbed by the incident occurring just a short distance from his nation's heartland. While the Abinader administration took some preliminary measures, such as closing the border with Haiti and issuing press releases condemning the assassination (Fils-Aime & Charles, 2021), these actions appeared to be more about presenting an image of concern than a genuine anxiety over the unfolding events in Haiti.

The response of the Dominican Republic's president to the assassination of the Haitian president raised eyebrows among many observers. It seemed as though he might have expected such an event. It is also possible that the orchestrator of the murder assured the Dominican president that he would not be affected. Given the powerful influence US officials hold on the Dominican government, one could not (or should not) overlook the potential implications of these connections.

In the months leading up to President Moïse's death, there were reports among local media outlets in Haiti of the newly installed Dominican president had treated his Haitian counterpart impolitely during his inauguration. These subtle cues were, regrettably, not detected by Haitian security officials. Perhaps they should have.

As we continue to examine the aftermath of the assassination, it is crucial to consider the potential roles and relationships between regional players and their influence on the events that transpired in Haiti. In doing so, we can begin to understand the broader context in which these events unfolded and the challenges that law enforcement and security forces faced in their attempts to maintain order and protect their nation's leaders.

There is no doubt in my mind that President's Moïse's death was a vast conspiracy. Despite the fact that many American officials have expressed their intent to investigate the events that transpired in Haiti on July 7, 2021, leading to the assassination of President Jovenel Moïse, the prevailing perception is that the president was left exposed and inadequately protected (Danticat, 2021). Soon after the news broke, there were suspicions that presidential security guards played a role in the assassination (Pannett et al., 2021). Surprisingly, not a single shot was fired by the presidential security guards, who are reputed to be well trained and prepared to protect the president at all costs. As someone who has first-hand experience training several of these individuals, it is puzzling to observe their failure to execute their duties during this critical incident. They had been trained to handle various scenarios, including potential intrusions into the presidential compound.

In 1997, the US established and trained a group of elite police officers, known as the CAT Team (Counter-Ambush/Counterterrorism Team), with the primary mission of protecting the Haitian president and his immediate family members. As the original leader of this team, I can attest to the high-quality training and the preparation that these officers received to face any potential threats to the president's safety and security. They were trained to prevent unauthorized access to the presidential palace. They learned how to eliminate the possibility of significant harm to the president or the Haitian presidency itself.

Besides the CAT Team, other high-level security forces within the Haitian National Palace, such as the Presidential Security Unit (PSU) and the National Palace Presidential Guard (NPRG),[3] were trained to neutralize

---

[3] The PSU, CAT, and NPRG are separate entities within the Haitian Secret Service. Dimitri Herard, whose name has been

potential threats against the president. These officers possess the expertise to detect, prevent, and thwart any attempts on the president's life, whether he is in his office, at home, or traveling. Protocols were in place to prevent incidents like the assassination of President Jovenel Moïse. The question remains: how could such a tragedy occur without a conspiracy at the highest level of the Haitian government, especially when one considers the US influence and control over the government under any conceivable scenario?

Granted, I lack concrete answers to the many questions surrounding this case. But I have my own suspicions and theories regarding the true motive behind the president's assassination. This work, I must admit, may not be the venue to divulge these thoughts.

The details surrounding the Haitian president's death remain largely unknown. Given the gravity of the situation, one would expect a significant amount of media curiosity and investigative zeal. The assassination of a president in his own home, particularly one from a friendly country, should have prompted journalists to conduct thorough investigations. They should have been tenacious in their pursuit of the truth, seeking to uncover the events that unfolded in Haiti, particularly considering

mentioned as the head of security at Haiti's presidential palace by the Washington Post, was in charge of the NPRG, which entity only oversees the residential security matters. See (Pannett et al., 2021).

the potential implications for other regional leaders. Unfortunately, this level of investigative journalism was not the norm, although there were a few commendable exceptions. Given this depressing reality, it is essential that we continue to question and even to scrutinize the circumstances of President Moïse's assassination. We must do so not only for the sake of the Haitian people but also for the broader implications that such an event has on regional stability and security. As new information comes to light, it is our collective responsibility to engage with this issue critically and demand transparency and accountability from all parties involved.

CHAPTER 8

THE MEDIA AND KIDNAPPED MISSIONARIES

The assassination of the Haitian president, Jovenel Moïse, has captured the media's attention. However, it did so only for a specific period. The media frenzy surrounding this case reached new heights after both the New York Times and CNN reported on the ongoing investigation, linking the alleged mastermind of the assassination, Joseph Badjo, to Haiti's current head of state, Ariel Henry.[4] Evidence points to a deep-rooted conspiracy surrounding Moïse's assassination, with revelations of phone conversations between Henry and Badjo shortly after the incident. The

---

[4] See these articles to learn more:
https://www.cnn.com/2022/02/08/americas/haiti-assassination-investigation-prime-minister-intl-cmd-latam/index.html;
https://www.nytimes.com/2021/09/14/world/americas/haiti-henry-moise-assassination.html

---

investigation into the president's death continues to unfold as we speak.

Besides the assassination, Haiti experienced a 7.2 magnitude earthquake on August 14, 2021, which claimed the lives of 2,200 people and injured over 12,200 more (Masciarelli, 2021; World Food Programme, 2021). This natural disaster brought Haiti to the forefront of both national and international news once again.

Remarkably, months after both the president's assassination and the devastating earthquake, Haiti continues to make headlines. It was unusual for the country to maintain such a sustained presence in the media, given that coverage often focuses on catastrophes, whether natural or man-made (Girard, 2010, p. 3). In fact, Haiti had largely been absent from the public eye since the 2004 coup d'état, with only sporadic appearances during crises such as hurricanes, food riots, and the 2010 earthquake (Girard, 2010).

The kidnapping of US missionaries had intensified media interest in Haiti. This situation, along with the ongoing investigations into Moïse's assassination and the earthquake's aftermath, has made Haiti a persistent topic of discussion in the media landscape. This extended media focus on Haiti presented an opportunity to delve deeper into the complexities of the country's political, social, and economic challenges. It is crucial that journalists and media outlets continue to examine and report on these critical issues, while also highlighting the resilience and strength of the Haitian people in the face of adversity.

Under normal circumstances, there is a discrepancy in media coverage of Haitian affairs. It is not a puzzling reality to note a lack of media interest in Haiti's political afflictions. As insinuated earlier, there had been a complete blackout on the ongoing political and economic crises in Haiti in recent years. For instance, there had been many atrocities, including gang-related massacres, in Haiti. Other tragic events had occurred in the country, including viral images showing people in Haiti being consumed by animals, such as pigs and dogs in broad daylight. Yet, global news media outlets have generally overlooked the plight of the Haitian people. Certainly, the reasons for this apparent disregard are unclear.

Since Jovenel Moïse assumed the presidency in late 2016, his administration has been plagued with a host of issues, including his alleged connections to notorious gang leaders. Despite the escalating violence and instability, Haiti largely remained a non-issue at the global stage. Most global media outlets have remained disengaged in Haitian affairs. They have failed to report on the increasingly volatile situation in the country; at least, they failed to do so adequately.

President Moïse had been deceased for more than a few months. The hype over the usual television rounds and meetings for the gallery at the United Nations over the need to collect more moneys to help Haitians after the August earthquake had subsided. Haiti had been, once again, placed on the shelves of the forgotten. But in

November 2021, something strange happened. The country was back in the global news cycle.

Haiti had suddenly captured international news media attention, with reporters from renowned news organizations flocking to the country. The reason behind this sudden resurgence of media interest in Haiti became apparent to me upon further investigation. A group of 17 US missionaries and their family members, I learned, had been kidnapped by the infamous "400 Mawozo" gang (Faiola, 2021).

This incident underscored a glaring inconsistency in media coverage of Haitian affairs. While Haitians have endured a kidnapping epidemic since early 2018, it took the abduction of US nationals to provoke widespread media attention. The focus on this incident highlights a potential bias in the international media's reporting of Haiti, suggesting that the suffering of the Haitian people alone may not be deemed "newsworthy" enough.

This discrepancy raises important questions about the role and responsibility of the media in reporting on global crises, particularly those affecting marginalized or underprivileged populations. It is crucial that media outlets strive for fair and balanced coverage. They must highlight not only incidents involving foreign nationals, but also the broader context of Haiti's ongoing challenges and the resilience of its people.

CHAPTER 9

THE UNSETTLING TRUTH OF HAITI'S MISERY

There is an unsettling reality behind the rise of kidnappings in Haiti. When I first learned about the extent of criminality in Haiti, I struggled to comprehend the underlying factors driving this alarming trend. The targeting of US nationals in a country that has been under a thinly veiled foreign occupation since 2004 seemed particularly perplexing. I assumed that such abductions would surely trigger a swift and decisive response from the US, dismantling the kidnapping industry in Haiti and putting an end to the reign of terror inflicted by local gangs.

However, the reality turned out to be far different from what I had expected. The kidnapped missionary group reportedly managed to escape their captors and trek several miles to freedom (Bottar et al., 2021; The Associated Press, 2021). This narrative, reminiscent of a

Hollywood action movie, appeared implausible given the ruthlessness of Haitian gangsters in recent years. It led me to suspect that there might be more to the story than meets the eye.

This suspicion raises essential questions about the role and influence of foreign powers in Haiti's ongoing crisis. Could the persistence of criminality in the country be linked to external forces that benefit from the instability? Might the circumstances of the missionaries' escape serve as a smokescreen for a more complex and far-reaching web of relationships between the gangsters, foreign entities, and perhaps even elements within the Haitian government?

These questions demand thorough investigation and honest reflection, as they hint at the possibility that the crisis in Haiti may not be entirely homegrown. Unraveling the intricate connections between local criminals, foreign interests, and political actors could be vital in identifying the true driving forces behind the violence and chaos that continue to plague the Haitian people. Ultimately, exposing these links and addressing the root causes of the crisis are important steps toward restoring peace, stability, and sovereignty to Haiti. It is important to examine the underlying causes of insecurity in that part of the world.

As I grappled with the puzzling escape of an entire group of US missionaries from the clutches of a notoriously brutal Haitian gang, a question arose: Who is behind the escalating criminality in Haiti, and who is financing these ruthless gangsters? The answer, it seemed, pointed toward the US. If not directly responsible, American officials have certainly turned a blind eye to the plight of the Haitian people, as various entities—including US businesses, politicians, and Haitian oligarchs—continue to profit from the ongoing chaos there.

The violence that defines Haiti's current state is frequently perceived through a narrow lens that attributes the pervasive insecurity to a uniquely Haitian problem (Marcelin, 2015). This perspective suggests that instability is a common issue for countries on the margins of the global system and those that are marginalized by it (Marcelin, 2015). However, it is important to recognize that the roots of Haiti's struggles can often be traced back to the US. The role of both local and global politics in exacerbating insecurity in Haiti cannot be overlooked.

Haiti's political destiny is inextricably linked to the foreign policies of the US, whether through formal or informal channels. Insecurity in Haiti has been weaponized as political leverage, with the US emerging as a prominent instigator of this instability. To understand the full scope of the problem, we must delve deeper into the complex web of interests and influences that contribute to the ongoing crisis in Haiti.

By unraveling this intricate network of connections, we can begin to uncover the true driving forces behind the violence and chaos that continue to afflict the Haitian people. Identifying and addressing these underlying causes is essential to pave the way for sustainable peace, stability, and sovereignty in Haiti. As we work to untangle these connections, we must remain vigilant and challenge any attempts to oversimplify or downplay the multifaceted nature of Haiti's struggles.

A complex web of insecurity and political interests is the roots of the turmoil that characterizes Haiti. In the past, the American government has exploited insecurity and drug trafficking to manipulate local politicians in Haiti. It is believed that elected officials were often lured into corruption and political misconduct by CIA operatives, who would then use this information to blackmail them into serving US interests. This tactic may explain why the US has rarely supported honest Haitians in positions of power.

While President Moïse's administration initially received the same support as his predecessor, Michel Martelly, the political landscape shifted during his tenure. Numerous allies of Moïse joined the opposition, resisting his plan to create a new constitution that would favor foreign entities. As a result, insecurity and political instability escalated in Haiti. Both pro- and anti-government factions were impacted by the insecurity, as they each had their own groups of hoodlums operating on the streets and targeting opposition leaders. Amidst this chaos, many of those opposing Moïse's plans found themselves sanctioned by the international community, including the US, France, and Canada.

In Haiti, politics and insecurity are inextricably linked, with insecurity often used as leverage to achieve or hinder political objectives. No foreign power is more deeply involved in Haitian politics than the US government. Over the past three decades, American officials have consistently influenced the socio-political trajectory of Haiti. This raises the possibility that the American government has played a role in perpetuating the current climate of insecurity in the country, either directly or indirectly, by supporting political instability, which also fosters an environment conducive to crime and violence.

The pervasive influence of the US in Haitian politics has led to a situation where the Haitian political class has become subservient to the whims of foreign interests. This lack of autonomy and the ensuing chaos can be traced back to 2004, when Haiti's political landscape began its downward spiral. To address the ongoing security crisis, it is essential to confront the complex web of interests and influences that contribute to the insecurity and political instability that continues to plague this Caribbean nation.

The US government's influence on Haitian politics cannot be understated. American officials have played a significant role in deciding who ascends to power and who is excluded from positions of authority in the country. This heavy-handed approach to Haitian politics is difficult to deny, though it has far-reaching implications for the Haitian people.

In the past, I held a distinct perspective on the origins of crime and insecurity in Haiti. As someone who has worked with various US entities, including individuals from the State Department, I initially believed that the US had good intentions in Haiti. This belief was reinforced by my first-hand experiences with the corrupt nature of many Haitian politicians, which made it easy to blame Haitians for their own troubles. I was not alone in holding this view.

Recent events, such as the assassination of President Jovenel Moïse, have forced me to reevaluate my assumptions about foreign roles in the chaos in Haiti.[5] The unwavering US support for those believed to be involved in Moïse's murder has raised concerns among many who are not blinded by ideological biases. Contrary to the belief held by some observers, the issue of crime in Haiti cannot be solely attributed to internal factors.

While the problem of insecurity is undoubtedly linked to ongoing social, economic, and political upheavals in the country, it is essential to recognize that the roots of this issue extend beyond Haiti's borders. In particular, the role of US foreign policy in shaping the Caribbean island's security landscape cannot be ignored. There is more to the

---

[5] I must mention that I offered to help Haiti, particularly the Haitian National Police, in their fight against criminality in Haiti. I have reached out to the proper police officials, proposing strategies to address the insecurity problem in the country. Although I am among an elite of highly trained and American-educated police officers with ties with the Haitian police, my offer to assist the police has consistently been turned down. Perhaps my worldview no longer jibes with that of those in power in Haiti. This turn of events has reinforced my apprehensions that the insecurity problem in Haiti is no coincidence. Rather, it is by design.

problem of insecurity than most people realize, although the nature of Haitian insecurity is often viewed from the lens of ongoing social, economic, and political ruptures (James, 2011).

Upon closer examination, it becomes apparent that the seeds of insecurity in Haiti are deeply intertwined with US foreign politics. The challenges faced by Haiti cannot be fully understood or addressed without acknowledging the impact of external forces, particularly those driven by the US. To tackle the crisis of insecurity in Haiti effectively, a comprehensive and nuanced approach is needed—one that considers the complex interplay between local and global actors and considers the role of US foreign policy in shaping the country's political landscape and security situation.

CHAPTER 10

A NATION GRIPPED BY FEAR

In December 2020, I made an impromptu visit to Haiti, a decision driven by both personal and professional motives. Despite the unsettling advice and concerns expressed by relatives and friends, I felt compelled to return to my homeland, which I held so dear to my heart. The urge to reconnect with my roots and to witness the current state of affairs in the country was too strong to ignore.

Another factor that fueled my determination to visit Haiti was my desire to support my former colleagues in the Haitian National Police (HNP).[6] I had crafted a strategic security plan designed to help law enforcement officials tackle the rising tide of kidnappings across the

---

[6] I joined the Haitian National Police in 1995. I am among the first leaders of the institution's most prestigious elite units, including Anti-riot police (CIMO), SWAT Team, Presidential Security (Haitian Secret Service), and CAT Team (Counter Ambush and Terrorism Team).

---

nation. My intention was to hand over this plan to the leaders of the civilian police force.

During my stay in Haiti, I experienced the harsh reality of the insecurity situation. The country was gripped by a pervasive atmosphere of fear and terror. Since the beginning of 2021, the capital city of Port-au-Prince and other major urban centers had been subjected to a relentless onslaught of crime, effectively placing them under a de facto state of siege.

The Haitian people, I observed, were living with an unparalleled sense of dread. Their daily existence was marred by abductions, armed robberies, sexual assaults, targeted killings, and a myriad of other violent offenses. While such criminal activity was not entirely unprecedented in Haiti, the current climate of despair and the palpable sense of lawlessness that permeated the country were truly disheartening.

The harrowing experiences of the Haitian population, caught in the crossfire of rampant criminality and struggling to navigate an increasingly volatile environment, painted a somber picture of a nation in crisis. It underscored the urgent need for effective intervention and support to address the complex web of challenges facing Haiti and its beleaguered people. But I felt powerless before the demise of my people.

The Haitian social landscape is in turmoil. The country has undergone a dramatic transformation in recent years. Since the summer of 2018, the nation has found itself increasingly under the sway of both local and international criminals. These mercenaries, driven by avarice and ambition, are willing to resort to any means necessary to achieve their ends. This precarious situation, orchestrated and perpetuated by certain factions within the international community, has served to undermine the Haitian state in a deeply insidious manner. The origins of this crisis can be traced back to 2004.

The situation deteriorated further under the auspices of the United Nations, with a turning point occurring in 2011 when the US effectively installed Michel Joseph Martelly as Haiti's president. Martelly, a man notorious for his moral shortcomings and debauched lifestyle, epitomized the concept of "legal bandits." Some observers regarded Martelly as "Haiti's second great disaster" post the 2010 earthquake, which claims the lives of so many Haitians and left over 700,000 people still homeless (Grandin, 2011). Yet, for reasons unknown, the American government, notably then Secretary of State, Hillary Clinton, saw Martelly as the best choice to lead Haiti, claiming that "we are behind him; we have a great deal of enthusiasm" (Grandin, 2011). This decision seemed to be a direct affront to the predominantly conservative Haitian populace.

The reason behind Washington's cavalier treatment of Haiti remains a subject of debate. Some argue that the relationship between the two countries is fundamentally influenced by racial dynamics that also characterize the US domestically. It could be difficult to refute that contention, considering the treatment Haitians received as opposed to other nations facing similar problems.

Faced with the ongoing insecurity crisis, Haiti finds itself as a republic besieged by a pernicious and thinly veiled form of racism. The very actors who proclaim themselves to be allies of the Haitian people have shown a callous disregard for their well-being and the future of their nation. It is as if there is a desire to see Haiti implode from within. The ultimate question remains: who stands to benefit from such a catastrophe?

CHAPTER 11

THE INTERNATIONAL COMMUNITY AND CRIMINALITY

Haitians have long been subject to the whims of foreign political and economic aggressors, many of whom are influenced by a community of individuals intent on punishing the Haitian people for the perceived sin their ancestors committed in 1804 by declaring Haiti an independent nation, free from the clutches of self-proclaimed champions of freedom. This paternalistic attitude towards the country and its people undermines even the most fundamental Haitian values, even in the subtlest ways.

Since 2004, Haiti has been subjected to a political and economic blockade, imposed out of contempt and intensified disdain for the Haitian people on the bicentennial of their independence from French colonization and brutal slavery. Both the French and the US orchestrated the 2004 coup, which was in part motivated because then President Jean-Bertrand Aristide started demanding reparations from the country's former colonizers, notably France (Democracy Now, 2022; Méheut et al., 2022). But this latest coup d'état was also a retaliatory act against the already beleaguered Haitian population. Of course, the interpretation of these events may be left to individual judgment.

At this point in Haiti's tumultuous political history, it is indubitable that the country is under a barely veil foreign occupation. The Haitian people are under the control of ordinary individuals who feign piety and wish to be perceived as virtuous and puritanical. This facade is far from the truth. Haiti longs for a democracy that may never materialize. A significant obstacle in the Haitian path towards progress is the pervasive and debilitating insecurity afflicting the population.

This widespread insecurity can be traced back to the influence of the international community, whose interests have shaped Haiti's political, social, and economic landscape. In this context, it becomes important to recognize and address the role of external forces in perpetuating the cycle of criminality and instability in Haiti. Only then can the nation begin to forge a path towards genuine progress and self-determination.

The involvement of foreign entities in Haiti's struggles, particularly in homeland security, is evident. It appears that these entities do not desire a free and self-reliant Haiti. Persistent waves of criminality have held the country back for decades. Haiti is currently beset by an unmatched level of indifference. Anxiety and unease can be felt throughout the nation.

While the state of fear prevalent in Haiti makes headlines around the world, including in US media, there seems to be a lack of genuine interest in helping Haitians extricate themselves from the grip of criminality plaguing their homeland. Any efforts made by Haitian officials are met with significant resistance from members of the so-called international community, most notably the US. One example of this lies in Haiti's inability to arm its security forces legally, which is a deliberate restriction.

Haitian security forces cannot arm themselves because of an arms embargo imposed on the country in the early 1990s. This unjust embargo, which caused great harm to the Haitian people (Farmer et al., 2003) resulted from a military coup against President Jean-Bertrand Aristide, which many believe, through covert actions in Haiti and with members of the notorious militia group known as FRAPH,[7] had been orchestrated by the American government through the Central Intelligence Agency (CIA) (Aristide & Richardson, 1994; Ives, 1994; Malone, 1997; Sanders, 2007; Whitney, 1996). Despite the embargo against Haiti, which was designed to devastate the country (Elliott, 2010; Hufbauer & Oegg, 2000; Mandelbaum, 1996; Sprague, 2012), numerous US manufactured

---

[7] The term FRAPH stands for Front for the Advancement and Progress of Haiti, which was a right-wing paramilitary group, which had been sponsored by the CAI and led by Emmanuel "Toto" Constant.

weapons have found their way onto Haitian ports and shores. This illicit arms trade occurs under the complicit watch of US officials.

To break the cycle of insecurity and criminality in Haiti, the international community, particularly the US, must reassess its role in the nation's struggles. Only through genuine support and cooperation can Haitians begin to address the root causes of their homeland's issues. This is the best way for the country to move towards a brighter, if not a more stable, future.

Arms smuggling is a significant issue confronting Haitian security officials. Disturbingly, US weaponry has found its way to Haiti, seemingly with the acquiescence of the US government. This situation is seemingly fueled by US patrons who benefit from official government policies that marginalize the Haitian people. Such policies have been established, implemented, maintained, and imposed, often to the advantage of US benefactors with interests in Haitian affairs.

The condescending attitude towards the Haitian people in the US has persisted for over three decades. The consequences of this relationship have severely damaged Haiti's national security, as there seems to be a constant aim to keep the country vulnerable. Haiti cannot defend itself against various attacks, both from within and outside its borders, which often originate directly or indirectly from the US and its allies.

It would not be far-fetched to say that Haiti has more adversaries than allies within the international community.

Yes, this statement may sound hyperbolic to some. But it is based on the evidence previously outlined. If there is a serious need to fix Haiti's woes, the country would have been better off by now. Not only America has the resources to help Haiti fixes itself, but Haitians also have the will power and the desire to do the same. How could we call Haiti's situation a failure—a state failure, at that—when there is intransigence on the part of those who have the means and the power to remediate it?

If there were failure in Haiti, it would be on America's side, for overtly or covertly, America rules over Haiti. Hence, Haiti is not a failed state. Rather, America is a failed colonial power, for American neocolonialists could not see that Haiti's shame is [actually] their own repugnance. The more they speak about Ukraine, the more they reveal to the world their ugliness inside and outside. The more Haitians realize that they must reclaim their ownership of their land. Granted, this is a sad deduction for me, considering that I consider myself a proud Haitian American living in the United States.

For years, those who claim to be friends of Haiti have actively worked to undermine the country's security at every opportunity. The current state of insecurity in Haiti can be traced back to the policies enacted by those who profess to be the allies of the Haitian people, notably the US. To address these challenges, it is crucial for the international community, especially the US, to reevaluate its role in Haiti's ongoing struggles. By fostering genuine support and collaboration, Haitians can begin to tackle the root causes of their nation's problems and work towards a more stable and secure future.

CHAPTER 12

REFUTING THE FAILED STATE ARGUMENT

Is Haiti a failed state? The answer is probably in the negative. However, the country's state is even direr than being a failed nation. The assassination of President Jovenel Moïse revealed a lot about the real status of the Haitian nation within the international community.

The most apparent reality is that Haiti is not a state in the true sense of the term "Statehood." Instead, Haiti is an occupied land, a former state, if you will, with America as its main tutor. Let us consider the aftermath of the president's assassination to illustrate that assertion.

Soon after Moïse's death, various people were arrested, including those who were at the scene of the murder. Many individuals who were not present at the scene had been arrested or had been considered fugitives, considering that they have remained at large. The Haitian national police instigated in investigation, which conclusion had been forwarded to the Haitian justice system for further actions. Yet, the FBI went to Haiti to investigate the crime. Under what authority, one may wonder? The answer is not clear, considering that no American citizen had been killed in the attacked at President Moïse's residence. In the same way, Jovenel Moïse, the only person reported to have died, was not an American citizen. Then, under what vestige of authority the American justice system is involved in the investigation? Then again, the answer is not clear.

Some potential suspects have been indicted and/or are currently awaiting trial. Some have been condemned, surprisingly by American courts for actions that took place in a supposed independent and foreign country. The mere fact that the United States proclaims its jurisdiction, not as an international court system, but rather acting on its own and for its own interests, is also indicative of the subservient nature of the relationship, which American officials seemingly hold over Haitian officials. Hence, to refer to Haiti as a failed state is an understatement, for Haiti is not even a state. Then, the question becomes: what is a state?

To define a state or a country, it is essential to consider various aspects and perspectives. Matthews and Kauzlarich (2007) provide a comprehensive framework for defining state crimes, which can be adapted to understand the nature of a state or a country. According to their framework, essential qualities of state criminality include the generation of harm to individuals, groups, or property (Matthews & Kauzlarich, 2007). Similar crimes include action or inaction by the state or its agencies, the relationship to an assigned or implied trust or duty of the state, the involvement of governmental entities, and the act being committed in the self-interest of the state or elite groups controlling the state (Matthews & Kauzlarich, 2007).

The definition of a state or country can vary across different contexts and disciplines. For instance, Rogers and Weller (2014) discuss the diverse definitions of state capacity indicators, emphasizing that the breakdown of the concept differs in views on the drivers of capacity rather than the definition itself. A state has its own characteristics (Rogers & Weller, 2014). Mahmood (2014) emphasizes the legislative aspect of defining terrorism in international law. The understanding is that states must enact laws to punish acts intended to provoke a state of terror in the public (in general) or specific groups or individuals (Mahmood, 2014). This legislative perspective adds another dimension to the definition of a state, as it involves the state's role in addressing and preventing certain actions within its jurisdiction.

One of the key facets of statehood is sovereignty. Sovereign countries, also known as states, possess several key characteristics that define their status as independent entities. These characteristics encompass political, economic, and social dimensions, which collectively contribute to their sovereignty and distinctiveness in the international system. None of these realities applies to

Haiti right now, a situation that has been exacerbated by the current political reality on the ground in Haiti. Not only Haiti, as a supposed state, has no agency, the Haitian people, as the sole source of legitimacy and sovereignty, have no say in the polity of their land, a land, which we have been told time and time again, that is independent.

It is vital to emphasize at the outset of this analysis that a sovereign country exhibits political autonomy and independence. It has the authority to govern itself. But it must do so without external interference.

A sovereign country must have the ability to make and enforce laws; it must be able to establish institutions; it must engage in diplomatic relations with other states. In the same way, the political structure and the influential domestic interest groups within a state can also influence its foreign policy preferences (Brown & James, 2018).

Economically, sovereign countries have the capacity to manage their own finances, including the ability to raise revenue, incur debt, and conduct trade with other nations. The economic stability and creditworthiness of a sovereign country are often evaluated through sovereign credit ratings, which can influence its cash flows, cost of capital, and access to financial markets (Aras & Öztürk, 2018). It is also worth noting that the characteristics of a country, such as its vulnerability index and economic stability, play a crucial role in determining its sovereign yields and bond spreads (Borrallo et al., 2016).

Social and institutional factors also contribute to the characteristics of a sovereign country. These factors include the presence of stable economies, access to financial markets, and the level of inequality and autocracy within the country (Kemme et al., 2021). The presence of state-owned enterprises and their efficiency characteristics can also be indicative of a country's economic structure and governance (Abramov et al., 2017).

Considering the explanations echoed throughout this opus thus far, there is no question about one reality. That is, Haiti is not a state, let alone a failed state. Haiti is simply an occupied land, a land that I characterize as the Palestine of the Caribbean. While the country has kept, whether by design or else, its initial nationhood characteristics, which place it in the realm of a state, in the actuality, Haiti does not function as such. Therefore, Haiti is neither a state nor does it behave as such.

As we wind up this discussion, let me echo that comparing Haiti to Palestine is, in no way, shape, or form, an attempt on my part to elevate Haiti or to diminish the struggle of the Palestinian people. This assertion was not concocted as an attempt to vilify one group to the detriment of another. However, it is a deliberate choice of a terminology, which—I am also convinced—describes the plight of the Haitian people to keep their dignity, their integrity, their identity, and their land in the face of relentless assaults from foreign entities, namely the United States, France, and Canada.[8]

---

[8] In making that statement, I am prepared for the consequences that may soon follow. However, I intend to *fight back*.

If you have been to Haiti or if you have spent times with Haitians, this book has taught you nothing new about the Haitian struggle. For a good portion of Haiti's history, Haitians have heard about their enemy but had never seen its face. The so-called enemy of Haiti has remained elusive for a long time. Haitians have always seen the faces of the so-called friends of Haiti. It all changed in 2010.

Since the powerful earthquake that shook the nation at its core and the international response to this tragedy, most Haitians are now aware of who their real enemy is. In fact, the enemy, if I could refer to the forces that are determined to keep Haiti in a perpetual state of misery, is no longer hidden. They no longer attempt to hide their identity. To our surprise, the enemy of Haiti is also those who, for years, have claimed to be the "friends of Haiti."

As was clear during the election of Michel Martelly, those Haitian haters, barring any other civilized qualifiers, are now well known to most and by most Haitians. They can fool no one in Haiti. Thus, their intentions are not hidden. Of course, they are behind media narratives designed to paint Haiti and Haitians with a broad stroke and under a particular light, which is often an unflattering projector. In my view, Haitians are effectively the Palestinians of the Western Hemisphere. Insecurity is used as a tool to contain Haiti and the Haitian people.

CONCLUSION

There is an unabashed disdain for Haitians. While the previous statement may sound like exaggeration to most, those who have live in Haiti and understand the dynamic between the Haitian people and others around the world know the level of discrimination and exclusion that mark the relation Haitians usually experience in the hand of those who proudly call themselves friends of Haiti. The overt contempt displayed by certain factions within the international community towards the Haitian people is both striking and unprecedented. But these individuals have made no attempt to conceal their disdain for the descendants of the first Black Republic in the New World. In fact, one has the impression that they take pride in harboring such animosity towards the Haitian people. The intensity of this contempt is unparalleled in the country's history.

Panels of self-proclaimed experts often convene under the auspices of the United Nations to express their vitriol towards the beleaguered Haitian population. Haiti has come to resemble a protectorate subject to the oversight of the United Nations. The nation's autonomy and right to self-determination have been reduced to mere formalities, which are readily undermined by officials placed in power to cater to the whims of influential entities within the United Nations. These entities often act under the influence of the US and its allies, most notably France and Canada.

In this context, Haiti is treated as a subjugated nation, with its citizens living under the control of white individuals who purport to champion democracy. Yet, their actions reveal an overt display of authoritarianism, hegemony, and unadulterated racism. This unparalleled animosity towards the Haitian people stands in stark contrast to the claims of recognizing their independence and equality under the principles of natural law.

There is an unprecedented disregard for Haiti. The country has been subjected to a level of disrespect by the international community that is unparalleled in the region. With limited options, Haitians are forced to adapt to their reality and accept the unacceptable. They must do so under the belief that unity is the only remedy for their beleaguered nation.

The true malignancy threatening Haiti's existence can be attributed to the contempt harbored by its so-called friends, including, but not limited to, France, the US, Canada, the Dominican Republic, and even the United Nations. These entities effectively wield the greatest influence over the country. These foreign organizations possess economic and political power that surpasses anything that Haitian heads of state or political leaders could ever imagine.

It is undeniable that Haiti is at the mercy of the international community. These entities have consolidated their power and influence under a syndicate of international miscreants and infamous profiteers known as the "Core Group." This alliance is by no means a recent development.

The predicament Haiti finds itself in is not just the result of internal struggles, but also the consequence of external forces with vested interests. Haiti has no self-determination. Haitians have no real agency over their own destiny. Every internal decision must be approved by the so-called *Blan* or the "White man." Even Haiti's police chief must be approved by a foreign power, notably the United States. Would you call Haiti a Sovereign State?

These international entities, by wielding significant power over Haiti's political and economic landscape, have shaped the nation's destiny to serve their own agendas. As a result, the Haitian people continue to suffer. They are unable to break free from the clutches of these external influences. Does that reality make Haiti a failed state? I will let you be the judge of that.

REFERENCES

Abi-Habib, M., & Kurmanaev, A. (2021, September 14). Haiti Prosecutor Says Evidence Links Prime Minister to President's Killing. *The New York Times.* https://www.nytimes.com/2021/09/14/world/america s/haiti-henry-moise-assassination.html

Abramov, A., Radygin, A., Entov, R., & Chernova, M. (2017). State ownership and efficiency characteristics. *Russian Journal of Economics, 3*(2), 129–157.

Anders, B. (2013). Tree-huggers and baby-killers: The relationship between NGOs and PMSCs and its impact on coordinating actors in complex operations. *Small Wars & Insurgencies, 24*(2), 278–294.

Aras, O. N., & Öztürk, M. (2018). *The Effect of the Macroeconomic Determinants on Sovereign Credit Rating of Turkey.*

Aristide, M., & Richardson, L. (1994). Haiti's popular resistance. *NACLA Report on the Americas, 27*(4), 30–36.

Bano, M. (2008). Contested claims: Public perceptions and the decision to join NGOs in Pakistan. *Journal of South Asian Development, 3*(1), 87–108.

Bazin, A., & Saintis, C. (2021). Rezistans Klimatik: Building Climate Change Resilience in Haiti through Educational Radio Programming. *Education and Climate Change: The Role of Universities*, 113–136.

Beatrice, O. K. (2019). How Sovereign Is a State From Foreign Intervention? Gambia as a Case Study. *International Journal of Law and Public Administration, 2*(2), 10–23.

Bebbington, A. J., Hickey, S., & Mitlin, D. C. (Eds.). (2007). *Can NGOs Make a Difference?: The Challenge of Development Alternatives*. Zed Books.

Black, M. E. (2013). *Pray for Peace. Prepare for War... And Stability Operations*. US Army War College.

Borrallo, F., Hernando, I., & Valles, J. (2016). *The effects of US unconventional monetary policies in Latin America*.

Bottar, A., WKSU, & The Associated Press. (2021, December 20). *Kidnapped Missionaries Escaped From Haitian Gang, Ohio Missionary Group Says*. WOSU News. https://news.wosu.org/news/2021-12-20/kidnapped-missionaries-escaped-from-haitian-gang-ohio-missionary-group-says

Brown, D., & James, P. (2018). The religious characteristics of states: Classic themes and new evidence for international relations and comparative politics. *Journal of Conflict Resolution, 62*(6), 1340–1376.

Buschschlüter, V. (2024, March 6). Haiti gang leader threatens "civil war" if PM does not resign. *BBC News*.

https://www.bbc.com/news/world-latin-america-68486536

Ceccorulli, M., & Coticchia, F. (2016). Italy's military interventions and new security threats: The cases of Somalia, Darfur and Haiti. *Contemporary Politics, 22*(4), 412–431.

Chauvet, L., & Collier, P. (2008). Aid and reform in failing states. *Asian-Pacific Economic Literature, 22*(1), 15–24.

Chu, V., & Luke, B. (2021). Understanding success in micro-enterprise development: Dimensions and misconceptions. *Public Administration and Development, 41*(2), 63–78.

Chu, V., & Luke, B. (2022). A participatory approach: Shifting accountability in microenterprise development. *Financial Accountability & Management, 38*(1), 3–28.

Ciorciari, J. D. (2022). Haiti and the Pitfalls of Sharing Police Powers. *International Peacekeeping,* 1–29.

Cockayne, J. (2014). The futility of force? Strategic lessons for dealing with unconventional armed groups from the UN's war on Haiti's gangs. *Journal of Strategic Studies, 37*(5), 736–769.

Danticat, E. (2021, July 14). The Assassination of Haiti's President. *The New Yorker.* https://www.newyorker.com/news/news-desk/the-assassination-of-haitis-president

Dargis, M. (2014, February 28). The Damage That Good Can Inflict. *The New York Times.* https://www.nytimes.com/2014/02/28/movies/fatal-assistance-about-relief-efforts-in-haiti.html

Deen, J., Von Seidlein, L., Luquero, F. J., Troeger, C., Reyburn, R., Lopez, A. L., Debes, A., & Sack, D. A. (2016). The scenario approach for countries considering the addition of oral cholera vaccination in cholera preparedness and control plans. *The Lancet Infectious Diseases, 16*(1), 125–129.

Democracy Now. (2022, May 23). *Ex-Ambassador Admits France & U.S. Orchestrated 2004 Coup in Haiti to Oust Aristide.* Democracy Now! https://www.democracynow.org/2022/5/23/headlines/ex_ambassador_admits_france_us_orchestrated_2004_coup_in_haiti_to_oust_aristide

Dent, D. (1999). *The Legacy of the Monroe Doctrine: A Reference Guide to U.S. Involvement in Latin America and the Caribbean* (First American Edition). Greenwood.

Diaz-Bonilla, E. (2022). *Haiti and its multiple tragedies: Much more needs to be done* (Vol. 26). Intl Food Policy Res Inst.

Elliott, K. A. (2010). Assessing UN sanctions after the cold war: New and evolving standards of measurement. *International Journal, 65*(1), 85–97.

Eriksen, S. S. (2011). 'State failure'in theory and practice: The idea of the state and the contradictions of state formation. *Review of International Studies, 37*(1), 229–247.

Exime, E., Pallú, N. M., Plein, C., & Bertolini, G. R. F. (2021). The role of international cooperation in the development of haitian agriculture against hunger and poverty. *Research, Society and Development, 10*(14), Article 14. https://doi.org/10.33448/rsd-v10i14.21864

Faiola, A. (2021, October 17). American missionaries and family members kidnapped in Haiti by '400 Mawozo' gang, groups say. *Washington Post.*

https://www.washingtonpost.com/world/2021/10/17/haiti-american-missionaries-kidnapped/

Farmer, P., Chomsky, N., & Kozol, J. (2005). *The Uses of Haiti* (Third edition). Common Courage Press.

Farmer, P., Fawzi, M. C. S., & Nevil, P. (2003). Unjust embargo of aid for Haiti. *The Lancet, 361*(9355), 420–423.

Feldmann, A. E., Lengyel, M., Malacalza, B., & Ramalho, A. (2011). Lost in translation: ABC cooperation and reconstruction in Haiti. *Journal of Peacebuilding & Development, 6*(3), 45–60.

Ferdous, J. (2014). Micro credit program of NGOs in poverty alleviation: An empirical study on some selected NGOs. *IOSR J Hum Soc Sci (IOSR-JHSS), 19*(9), 26–35.

Fils-Aime, J., & Charles, J. (2021, July 7). Police kill 4 suspects after assassination of Haiti President Jovenel Moïse. *The Atlanta Journal-Constitution.* https://www.ajc.com/news/nation-world/official-haiti-president-jovenel-moise-assassinated-at-home/JZNPJ6KTJZBCDHWYX32TII2FJI/

Fischer, S. (2004). *Modernity Disavowed: Haiti and the Cultures of Slavery in the Age of Revolution* (Illustrated edition). Duke University Press Books.

Gallón, N., Rivers, M., & Dupain, E. (2022, February 8). *Haitian Prime Minister involved in planning the President's assassination, says judge who oversaw case.* CNN. https://www.cnn.com/2022/02/08/americas/haiti-assassination-investigation-prime-minister-intl-cmd-latam/index.html

Geggus, D. P., & Fiering, N. (Eds.). (2009). *The World of the Haitian Revolution* (Illustrated edition). Indiana University Press.

Ghachem, M. W. (2012). *The Old Regime and the Haitian Revolution.* Cambridge University Press. https://doi.org/10.1017/CBO9781139050173

Gilderhus, M. T. (2006). The Monroe Doctrine: Meanings and Implications. *Presidential Studies Quarterly, 36*(1), 5–16. https://doi.org/10.1111/j.1741-5705.2006.00282.x

Girard, P. (2010). *Haiti: The Tumultuous History - From Pearl of the Caribbean to Broken Nation: The Tumultuous History - From Pearl of the Caribbean to Broken Nation* (First edition). St. Martin's Griffin.

Gould, L. A. (2014). Exploring gender-based disparities in legal protection, education, health, political empowerment, and employment in failing and fragile states. *Women & Criminal Justice, 24*(4), 279–305.

Grandin, G. (2011, May 4). *Martelly: Haiti's second great disaster.* Al Jazeera. https://www.aljazeera.com/opinions/2011/5/4/martelly-haitis-second-great-disaster

Gugerty, M. K. (2008). The effectiveness of NGO self-regulation: Theory and evidence from Africa. *Public Administration and Development: The International Journal of Management Research and Practice, 28*(2), 105–118.

Hameiri, S. (2007). Failed states or a failed paradigm? State capacity and the limits of institutionalism. *Journal of International Relations and Development, 10*, 122–149.

Hendel, N., Korotkyi, T., & Yedeliev, R. (2022). Human Rights NGOs and Humanitarian NGOs. In *International Conflict and Security Law* (pp. 813–837). Springer.

Howard, D. (2007). Development, racism, and discrimination in the Dominican Republic. *Development in Practice*, *17*(6), 725–738.

Hufbauer, G. C., & Oegg, B. (2000). Targeted sanctions: A policy alternative. *Law & Pol'y Int'l Bus.*, *32*, 11.

Ioanes, E. (2024, March 12). *Haiti's prime minister is out. Here's how it got so bad.* Vox. https://www.vox.com/world-politics/2024/3/12/24098422/haiti-prime-minister-ariel-henry-resigns-gang-violence-g9

Ives, K. (1994). The unmaking of a President. *NACLA Report on the Americas*, *27*(4), 16–29.

James, E. C. (2003). *The Violence of Misery: "Insecurity" in Haiti in the "Democratic" Era* [Thesis, Havard University]. https://www.proquest.com/openview/f39c6856279c8c7c624131a17df9e978/1?pq-origsite=gscholar&cbl=18750&diss=y

James, E. C. (2009). Neomodern Insecurity in Haiti and the Politics of Asylum. *Culture, Medicine, and Psychiatry*, *33*(1), 153–159. https://doi.org/10.1007/s11013-008-9125-z

James, E. C. (2011). Haiti, Insecurity, and the Politics of Asylum. *Medical Anthropology Quarterly*, *25*(3), 357–376. https://doi.org/10.1111/j.1548-1387.2011.01165.x

Jessop, B. (2015). Crises, crisis-management and state restructuring: What future for the state? *Policy & Politics*, *43*(4), 475–492.

John, T., Ogunbayo, M., & Rios, M. (2024, March 5). *Haiti's prime minister lands in Puerto Rico, official says, as gangs rampage at home.* CNN. https://www.cnn.com/2024/03/05/americas/haiti-violence-prime-minister-henry-intl-latam/index.html

Kemme, D. M., Parikh, B., & Steigner, T. (2021). Inequality, autocracy, and sovereign funds as determinants of foreign portfolio equity flows. *Journal of Financial Research, 44*(2), 249–278.

Killion, C. M., Sloand, E., Gary, F. A., Glass, N., Dennis, B. P., Cesar Muller, N., Hassan, M., Callwood, G. B., & Campbell, D. W. (2018). Culturally anchoring an intervention for gender-based violence. *International Journal of Health Promotion and Education, 56*(2), 85–94. https://doi.org/10.1080/14635240.2017.1415766

Kolstø, P. (2006). The sustainability and future of unrecognized quasi-states. *Journal of Peace Research, 43*(6), 723–740.

Lewis, J. A. (2004). Modernity Disavowed: Haiti and the Cultures of Slaves in the Age of Revolution. *History: Reviews of New Books, 33*(1), 19–20. https://doi.org/10.1080/03612759.2004.10526397

Limoncelli, K. E., Mellow, J., & Na, C. (2020). Determinants of intercountry prison incarceration rates and overcrowding in Latin America and the Caribbean. *International Criminal Justice Review, 30*(1), 10–29.

Logie, C. H., Daniel, C., Ahmed, U., & Lash, R. (2017). 'Life under the tent is not safe, especially for young women': Understanding intersectional violence among internally displaced youth in Leogane, Haiti. *Global*

Health Action, 10(sup2), 1270816.
https://doi.org/10.1080/16549716.2017.1270816

Mahmood, M. S. (2014). A Quest for Defining Terrorism in International Law: The Emerging Consensus. *Journal of International Studies, 10*, 77–93. https://e-journal.uum.edu.my/index.php/jis/article/view/7949

Malone, D. (1997). Haiti and the international community: A case study. *Survival, 39*(2), 126–146.

Mandelbaum, M. (1996). Foreign policy as social work. *Foreign Aff., 75*, 16.

Marcelin, L. H. (2015). Violence, Human Insecurity, and the Challenge of Rebuilding Haiti: A Study of a Shantytown in Port-au-Prince. *Current Anthropology, 56*(2), 230–255. https://doi.org/10.1086/680465

Masciarelli, A. (2021). *Emergency Situation Report #3* (p. 3). World Food Programme. https://reliefweb.int/report/haiti/wfp-haiti-emergency-situation-report-3-3-september-2021

Matthews, R. A., & Kauzlarich, D. (2007). State crimes and state harms: A tale of two definitional frameworks. *Crime, Law and Social Change, 48*, 43–55.

Méheut, C., Porter, C., Gebrekidan, S., & Apuzzo, M. (2022, May 20). Demanding Reparations, and Ending Up in Exile. *The New York Times*. https://www.nytimes.com/2022/05/20/world/americas/haiti-aristide-reparations-france.html

Nordin, N. N. H., Husin, W. N. W., & Salleh, M. Z. (2022). Challenges in United Nations Peacekeeping Operations. *International Journal of Social Science Research, 10*(1), Article 1. https://doi.org/10.5296/ijssr.v10i1.19141

Olivier, D. (2021). The Political Anatomy of Haiti's Armed Gangs: In Port-au-Prince, botched NGO and military inventions have fragmented urban space, triggering an explosive proliferation of violent armed groups. *NACLA Report on the Americas, 53*(1), 83–87.

Pannett, R., Merancourt, W., & Schmidt, S. (2021). Mystery surrounds suspected mastermind of Haiti presidential assassination plot. *Washington Post, NA.* https://link.gale.com/apps/doc/A668240511/AONE?u=anon~1372f574&sid=googleScholar&xid=fd668b73

Peck, R. (Director). (2013, May 6). *Assistance mortelle* [Documentary]. ARTE, Canal Overseas Productions, Centre national du cinéma et de l'image animée (CNC).

Pillet, A. (1914). The Monroe Doctrine. *The ANNALS of the American Academy of Political and Social Science, 54*(1), 131–133.

Pintor, M. P., Suhrcke, M., & Hamelmann, C. (2023). The impact of economic sanctions on health and health systems in low-income and middle-income countries: A systematic review and narrative synthesis. *BMJ Global Health, 8*(2), e010968.

Ponsar, F., Ford, N., Van Herp, M., Mancini, S., & Bachy, C. (2009). Mortality, violence and access to care in two districts of Port-au-Prince, Haiti. *Conflict and Health, 3*(1), 1–6.

Porter, C., Crowley, M., & Méheut, C. (2021, July 7). Haiti's President Assassinated in Nighttime Raid, Shaking a Fragile Nation. *The New York Times.* https://www.nytimes.com/2021/07/07/world/americas/haiti-president-assassinated-killed.html

Rebok, S. (2009). La Révolution de Haïti vue par deux personnages contemporains: Le scientifique prussien Alexander von Humboldt et l'homme d'état américain Thomas Jefferson. *French Colonial History, 10*(1), 75–95. https://doi.org/10.1353/fch.0.0022

Rodrigues, G. M. (2015). Regional implementation of peacekeeping: Notes and lessons from the Brazilian experience in the MINUSTAH. *Perspectives on Peacekeeping and Atrocity Prevention: Expanding Stakeholders and Regional Arrangements*, 145–158.

Rogers, M. Z., & Weller, N. (2014). Income taxation and the validity of state capacity indicators. *Journal of Public Policy, 34*(2), 183–206.

Ryfman, P. (2007). Non-governmental organizations: An indispensable player of humanitarian aid. *International Review of the Red Cross, 89*(865), 21–46.

Saeng Outhay, O. (2015). *The influence of Non-Governmental Organisations (NGOs) on primary education policy in Laos.*

Sanders, R. (2007). The Coup-Installed Regime and its Reign of Terror.". *Press for Conversion, 60*, 7–9.

Sanon, E., Goodman, J., & Coto, D. (2024, March 5). *Haitian PM arrives in Puerto Rico after long absence as he struggles to get home to quell violence.* AP News. https://apnews.com/article/haiti-violence-prison-break-curfew-0116d2ebac1b14a587baa176818055cb

Sanon, M.-A., Mohammed, S. A., & McCullagh, M. C. (2014). Definition and management of hypertension among Haitian immigrants: A qualitative study. *Journal of Health Care for the Poor and Underserved, 25*(3), 1067.

Sauter, M. (2022). A Shrinking Humanitarian Space: Peacekeeping Stabilization Projects and Violence in Mali. *International Peacekeeping*, 1–26.

Schuberth, M. (2015). A transformation from political to criminal violence? Politics, organised crime and the shifting functions of Haiti's urban armed groups. *Conflict, Security & Development*, *15*(2), 169–196.

Schuller, M. (2007). Invasion or Infusion? Understanding the Role of NGOs in Contemporary Haiti. *Journal of Haitian Studies*, *13*(2), 96–119. https://www.jstor.org/stable/41715359

Schuller, M. (2009). Gluing Globalization: NGOs as Intermediaries in Haiti. *PoLAR: Political and Legal Anthropology Review*, *32*(1), 84–104. https://doi.org/10.1111/j.1555-2934.2009.01025.x

Sillah, A. B., & Adesopo, A. (2022). Non-Governmental Organisations and Health Service Delivery in The Gambia: A Case Study of The Hands-On-Care Clinic. *East African Journal of Health and Science*, *5*(1), 344–368.

Sørensen, G. (1999). Sovereignty: Change and continuity in a fundamental institution. *Political Studies*, *47*(3), 590–604.

Sprague, J. (2012). Paramilitaries in Haiti. *Monthly Review*, *64*(4), 24.

Tantua, B., & Isukul, A. (2022). The Failed State Syndrome and the Nigerian Narrative. *Wilberforce Journal of the Social Sciences (WJSS)*, *7*(2), 92–108. https://doi.org/10.36108/wjss/2202.70.0260

The Associated Press. (2021, December 20). Missionaries who were kidnapped in Haiti escaped from their abductors, aid group says. *NPR*.

https://www.npr.org/2021/12/20/1065923822/missio
naries-who-were-kidnapped-in-haiti-escaped-from-their-
abductors-aid-group-

U. S. Mission Haiti. (2018, February 21). *Ambassador Michele
Sison presented credentials to President Jovenel Moise*. U.S.
Embassy in Haiti.
https://ht.usembassy.gov/ambassador-sison-
credentials/

UN Office for the Coordination of Humanitarian Affairs.
(2022, July 9). *Haiti: Impact of the deteriorating security
situation on humanitarian access: Background note - 8 July 2022*.
https://reliefweb.int/report/haiti/haiti-impact-
deteriorating-security-situation-humanitarian-access-
background-note-8-july-2022

Vahedi, L., Bartels, S. A., & Lee, S. (2021). 'Even
peacekeepers expect something in return': A qualitative
analysis of sexual interactions between UN peacekeepers
and female Haitians. *Global Public Health*, *16*(5), 692–705.
https://doi.org/10.1080/17441692.2019.1706758

Van Engeland, A. (2016). Contextualisation of
Humanitarian Assistance and its Shortcomings in
International Human Rights Law. *Israel Law Review*,
49(2), 169–195.

van Veen, E. (2016). *Improving Security and Justice Programming
in Fragile Situations*.

Vinaygathasan, T., & Pallegedara, A. (2014). Impacts of
NGO intervention on poverty reduction: An empirical
evidence from rural Sri Lanka. *International Journal of
Sustainable Economy*, *6*(3), 288–301.

Whitney, K. M. (1996). SIN, FRAPH, and the CIA: US
covert action in Haiti. *Sw. JL & Trade Am.*, *3*, 303.

World Food Programme. (2021, September 3). *WFP Haiti: Emergency Situation Report #3, 3 September 2021*. https://reliefweb.int/report/haiti/wfp-haiti-emergency-situation-report-3-3-september-2021

Zanotti, L. (2010). Cacophonies of Aid, Failed State Building and NGOs in Haiti: Setting the stage for disaster, envisioning the future. *Third World Quarterly, 31*(5), 755–771. https://doi.org/10.1080/01436597.2010.503567

INDEX

ABOUT THE AUTHOR

BEN WOOD JOHNSON, Ph.D.
Dr. Johnson is an author, educator, and philosopher. He is a social observer. He is a multidisciplinary researcher. He writes about philosophy, legal theory, public and foreign policy, education, politics, ethics, race, and crime.

Dr. Johnson holds a doctorate in educational leadership, a master's degree in political science, a master's degree in public administration, a master's degree in criminal justice, and a bachelor's degree in criminal justice. He has worked in law enforcement.

Dr. Johnson is fluent in many languages, including but not limited to Creole, French, English, Spanish, Portuguese, and Italian. He enjoys reading, poetry, painting, and music. You can contact Dr. Johnson by email at: benwoodpost@gmail.com.

Other Info

This book was published and printed by Tesko Publishing for Ben Wood Educational Consulting, LLC (BWEC, LLC). If you wish to contact Tesko Publishing, you can do so by referring to the information listed below.

BWEC, LLC/Eduka Solutions:

Post Office: 330 W. Main Street Unit #214
Middletown, Pennsylvania 17057

Email: tkpubhouse@gmail.com

TESKO PUBLISHING

www.ingramcontent.com/pod-product-compliance
Lightning Source LLC
Chambersburg PA
CBHW031437270326
41930CB00007B/751